W9-CAF-471

Property of Sunrise School

Read-About® Geography

Types of Maps

By Mary Dodson Wade

Consultant
Jeanne Clidas, Ph.D.
National Reading Consultant
and
Professor of Reading, SUNY Brockport

Children's Press®
A Division of Scholastic Inc.
New York   Toronto   London   Auckland   Sydney
Mexico City   New Delhi   Hong Kong
Danbury, Connecticut

Designer: Herman Adler Design
Photo Researcher: Caroline Anderson
The artwork on the cover shows four different types of maps. Clockwise
from upper left, road map, weather map, industry map, and elevation map.

Library of Congress Cataloging-in-Publication Data

Wade, Mary Dodson.
  Types of maps / by Mary Dodson Wade.
     p. cm. — (Rookie read-about geography)
Includes index.
Summary: Introduces different types of maps and how they are used,
including those that show how to get to a place and those that show what
you will find when you arrive.
  ISBN 0-516-22721-1 (lib. bdg) 0-516-27768-5 (pbk.)
  1. Maps—Juvenile literature. [1. Maps.] I. Title. II. Series.
  GA105.6 .W34 2003
  912—dc21
                                           200201156

Did you know there
are many different kinds
of maps?

A map can show you how to get to a place you want to visit. It can also tell you what you might find when you get there.

Road maps help drivers find their way.

Road maps have lines that stand for roads and highways.

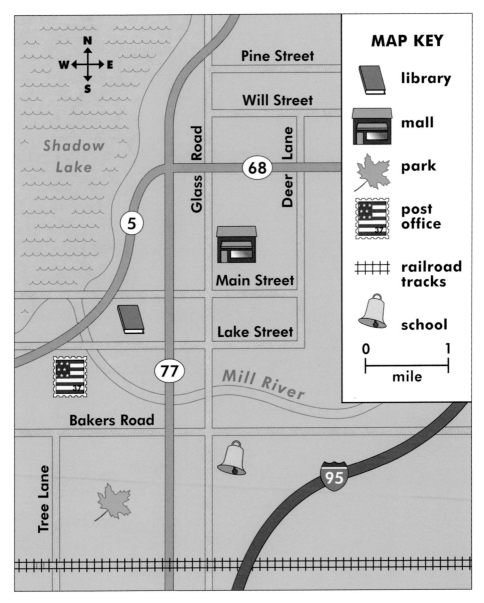

MAP KEY

📘	library
🏬	mall
🍁	park
📮	post office
╫╫╫	railroad tracks
🔔	school

0 ——————— 1
mile

Pine Street
Will Street
Shadow Lake
Glass Road
Deer Lane
68
5
Main Street
Lake Street
77
Mill River
Bakers Road
Tree Lane
95

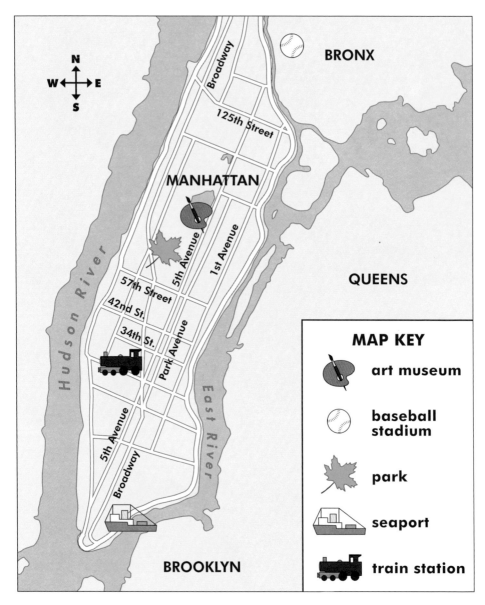

N
W ← → E
S

BRONX

Broadway

125th Street

MANHATTAN

5th Avenue

1st Avenue

QUEENS

Hudson River

57th Street

42nd St.

34th St.

Park Avenue

East River

5th Avenue

Broadway

BROOKLYN

MAP KEY

art museum

baseball stadium

park

seaport

train station

City maps help people find their way around cities.

This map shows New York City. Can you point to the art museum (MYOO-see-uhm) and the baseball stadium?

World maps show the
whole world.

On this map, green is
the color of land. Blue is
the color of oceans, rivers,
and lakes.

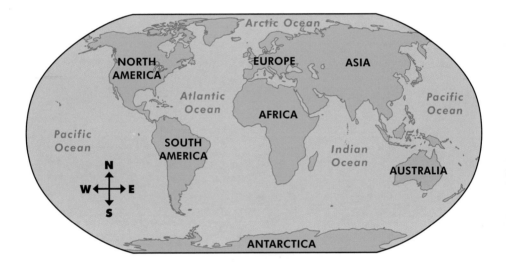

11

A map of the United States shows the outlines of the states.

Most of the states touch
each other. Two states do
not touch each other.
Can you name them?

MAP KEY

3,000–6,000 ft.
1,500–3,000 ft.
600–1,500 ft.
300–600 ft.
0–300 ft.

ATLANTIC
OCEAN

San Juan

PUERTO RICO

N
W E
S

Caribbean Sea

Some maps are elevation (el-uh-VAY-shuhn) maps. They use colors to show high and low places.

Low places are green on this map. Higher places are yellow. Very high places are brown.

Important buildings are
sometimes drawn on maps.

The White House

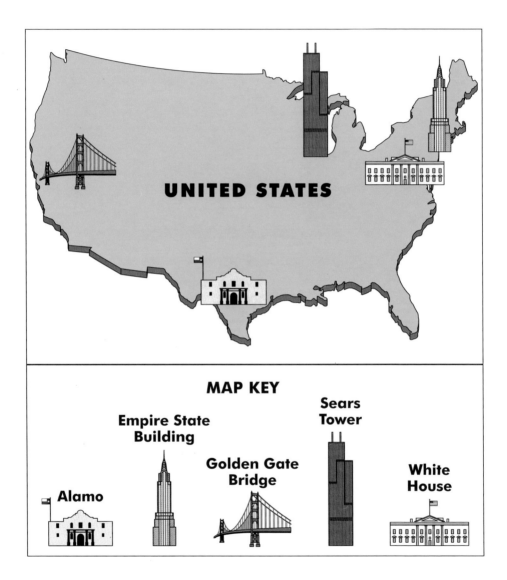

UNITED STATES

MAP KEY

Alamo

Empire State
Building

Golden Gate
Bridge

Sears
Tower

White
House

20

The White House is in
Washington, D.C.

The Empire State Building
is in New York City.

The Alamo is in San
Antonio, Texas.

Can you point to these
buildings on this map?

Maps sometimes show where animals live. Can you name the animals you see here?

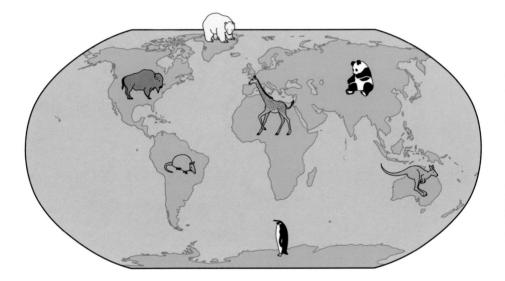

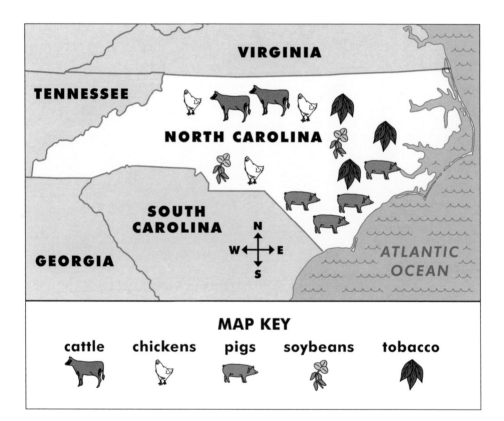

MAP KEY

cattle   chickens   pigs   soybeans   tobacco

Maps can show where foods grow. A map may have pictures of soybeans, chickens, and cows.

Some maps show where
things took place in the
past.

This map shows the path
two explorers took
on their trip out west.
Explorers are people
who travel to new places.

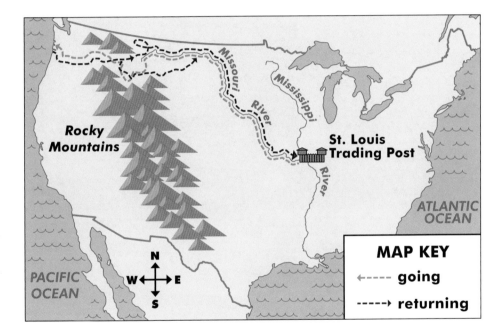

Rocky
Mountains

Missouri River

Mississippi River

River

St. Louis
Trading Post

PACIFIC
OCEAN

ATLANTIC
OCEAN

N
W — E
S

MAP KEY

←----- going

-----→ returning

There are so many
different kinds of maps.

Which one will you use
the next time you want
to know about a place?

Words You Know

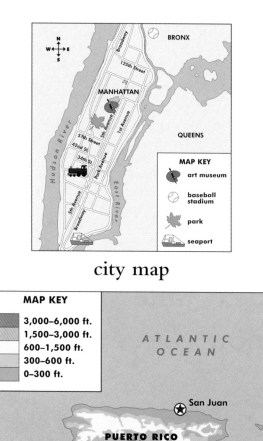

city map

elevation map

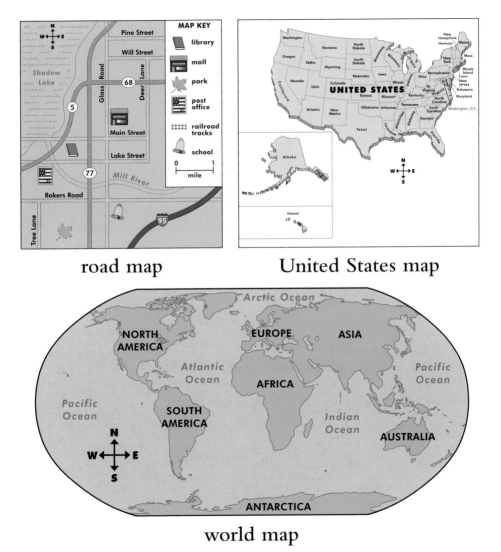

road map

United States map

world map

31

Index

About the Author

Mary Dodson Wade spent 25 years as an elementary school teacher, but she has been writing even longer than that, starting with poems as a child. She has had more than 20 books published. Mary and her husband live in Houston, Texas, and love to travel.

Photo Credits

Photographs © 2003: Corbis Images/Richard Ransier: 3; Peter Arnold Inc./Martha Cooper: 12; Photo Researchers, NY: 28 (Grantpix), 4 (Larry L. Miller), 19 (Joe Sohm).

Maps by XNR Productions